ANDES

TOMAŽ ŠALAMUN

Andes

by Tomaž Šalamun

Translated by Jeffrey Young and Katarina Vladimirov Young

Black Ocean
Boston - Detroit - Chicago

Black Ocean
P.O. Box 52030
Boston, MA 02205
blackocean.org

Cover Art and Design by Abby Haddican | abbyhaddican.com

Book Design by Nikkita Cohoon | nikkita.co

ISBN 978-1-939568-18-2

Library of Congress Cataloging-in-Publication Data

Names: Šalamun, Tomaž, author. | Young, Jeffrey, 1968- translator. |
    Young, Katarina Vladimirov, translator.
Title: Andes / Tomaž Šalamun ; translated from the Slovenian by
    Jeffrey Young and Katarina Vladimirov Young, with the author.
Description: First edition. | Boston : Black Ocean, 2016.
Identifiers: LCCN 2016027531 | ISBN 9781939568182 (hardcover :
    alk. paper)
Subjects: LCSH: Šalamun, Tomaž--Translations into English.
Classification: LCC PG1919.29.A2 A6 2016 | DDC 891.8/415--dc23
LC record available at https://lccn.loc.gov/2016027531

FIRST EDITION

CONTENTS

II

III

IV

V

NOTES ON THE TRANSLATION OF TOMAŽ ŠALAMUN'S *ANDES*

Great poets/foretell their own deaths in a single line.
— Tomaž Šalamun, from his book *Amerika* (1973)

Clear and sweet is my soul, and clear and sweet is all that is not my soul.
—Walt Whitman, "Song of Myself" (1855)

But my soul is a fire that suffers if it does not blaze.
—Stendhal, quoted by Albert Camus in the introduction to *L'Envers et l'endroit* (1958)

This translation, like most of Tomaž Šalamun's work published in English to date, was born from a collaborative effort with the author. Sadly, it is also the last translation of an original manuscript that he would complete and authorize before his death, in December 2014, at the age of 73.

Our cooperation began in sunnier days, during summer 2012, as an offer to help him prepare rough translations of his poems in English. Since starting work on a documentary about Šalamun earlier that year, I could see how busy he was with all manner of literary activities and obligations. It would have been impossible for me to make this offer were it not for the happy fact of my marriage to the artist Katarina Vladimirov, who was born and raised in Šalamun's adopted hometown of Ljubljana. Though, as Šalamun told us, it was more her training and instincts as a painter than their shared mother tongue that gave him confidence that we could handle the task.

Being a native speaker, as we would soon discover, would have its limits, as Šalamun's language in *Andes* seeps beyond the borders of textbook and colloquial Slovenian to include a mix of neologisms and nonsense words (some we have rendered, however awkwardly, into English, others we have left in the impenetrable original), irregularities in grammar and syntax, and the occasional word or expression from the all-but-forgotten Italo-Slavic argot spoken in colorful variations up and down what was once the coast of Yugoslavia—from Šalamun's original hometown of Koper (as the seagull flies just minutes from the Italian border and his mother's ancestral home of Trieste) to his beloved Dalmatia and its magical islands of timeless, primal beauty.

Šalamun was many things, and one of them was certainly a Yugoslav, or more specifically, a cosmopolitan southern Slav native to the windswept and sun-blessed coastline of the Adriatic, with its pearly outposts of Venetian culture and mercantilism wedged between the elemental mysteries of water, earth, and sky. "*Sono Slavo Dalmata /* a son of Venice," Šalamun writes in *Andes*, in what may be his most straightforward self-declaration. References to the Yugoslavia of Šalamun's memory—from its specific foods and terms of endearment to its rivers, artists, secret police, to Tito—make appearances throughout *Andes*.

For authenticity's sake we deliberately left untouched words such as *potica* (Slovenian, a traditional holiday cake) and *džulbastija* and *tufahija* (Bosnian: a meat stew, a kind of candied apple). While older readers in Slovenia may appreciate the obscure Yugoslav references Šalamun peppers throughout *Andes*, most of his native readership will find these to be as enigmatic as Glagolitic script and as incomprehensible to them as to people in the United States or elsewhere.

Even using everyday language, Šalamun is able within *Andes* to liberate words from surface connotations and points of reference: stripped of context, or forced into new contexts, their meaning can seem to hum outside their borders. Sentences often break down into component parts and appear as staccato fragments of expression. As with a cracked mosaic, there is the sense that you are seeing only part of the picture. Or to say it another way: Šalamun's language in *Andes* can appear like a half-eaten trail of popcorn, or a segmented Ariadne's thread that you follow into the labyrinth, hoping it will lead you out from the maze. What is this labyrinth? Where does it go? This may well have been Šalamun's question to himself.

When we first began work on *Andes*, Šalamun gave us some straightforward advice: "Be as literal as possible, and don't look for any meanings."

This was invaluable to us as translators, and it could serve well the reader who steps into the world of memories, dreams, and visions that Šalamun conjures within this book. There is much that is happening inside *Andes*, and much of it is strange the way dreams are strange and life is strange. One thing is certain: whatever is happening in these poems, it is happening *inside the language.* It is the language itself that takes you into this world, where rules of grammar and syntax can, without warning, fold in on themselves, reconfigure, and like an enchanted origami creature take shape and fly away.

There are places when the more flexible nature of English may moot the effect that Šalamun's creations are having in the original. It's worth pointing out that not all of these are radical. For example, in many places in *Andes* (and in many of his poems), Šalamun uses the diminutive form of words much more often than is generally common in Slovenian. "Little" "small" or "tiny" rarely do justice to the sound and at times awkwardness of the original, as they lose not only their child-like quality but the sharper contrast in language between the innocence such words evoke and the often disturbing imagery of death and war (and their intimations), natural disasters, and the many other dark visions that take shape within this book.

Happily, there is also joy inside *Andes*, and light, and wonderment, humor, and seemingly frivolous moments that share the space with lyrical expressions of freedom, power, rebellion, and love. But these are usually short-lived respites, often encased in just a few short lines, and much of what could be called happiness in *Andes* has the quality of daydreams or nostalgia—fleeting, uncertain, illusory.

Nostalgia permeates *Andes* like mist. There is a palpable longing for lost times, people and places, and for dreams and visions that slip through the mind of an ageing man, "a frog with

/ a mouth," as Šalamun writes in the poem "David Schubert" in an oblique reference to himself. There is much that has the air of autobiography inside *Andes*, although Šalamun was master at blurring the line between life and art, or at fusing the lines in the way that two streams come together to form a more powerful flow. The level of subjectivity in *Andes* is so high that it is seldom possible to state definitively that any one line or poem "means" this or that one thing. Šalamun's language inhabits multiple levels of existence—it is a witches' brew of fragments, where the mundane mixes with the monstrous. Šalamun melds all of this polyphony through language into a "reality" that can, I believe, be read as a kind of unabridged autobiography of the many states of his mental experience.

It is certainly true that, as it is throughout his poetry, many of the names appearing in *Andes* refer to actual people who were dear to Šalamun in his life, e.g., his wife, mother, and sister Katarina; school friends and his music teacher, Vladimir Lovec, from Koper; and other artists and friends from the days of Yugoslavia. As in life, new memories mix with old, and several poems in *Andes* mention younger American poets who were Šalamun's recent students, new friends, and translators.

Specific place names that relate to Šalamun's life also appear inside *Andes* and form part of its imaginative terrain. While it is not my intention (nor within my ability) to decode the many references within this book, I think it worthwhile to mention that the words "Zone B" and "Zone A" in "The Ravine" are not an exercise in mental abstraction but refer very specifically to the two divisions of the Free Territory of Trieste that existed for nearly a decade after WWII. Koper, as the de facto capital of Zone B, was occupied and administered by the Yugoslav People's Army, and Šalamun spent his formative childhood years on this front line of the Cold War.

Several of the other "characters" in *Andes* derive from books that Šalamun appears to have been reading at the time. *Ghost Train through the Andes* gives the volume its title, and its author, Michael Jacobs, is referenced in several poems. The artist and enfant terrible Jean-Michel Basquiat is another of the shadow-personages that transmigrates into *Andes* (the ghost of his carnal self-destruction seeming to tempt the poet with the proposition that, even in old age, it is better to burn out than fade away). Other cameo appearances include the kindred spirits of Renaissance painters and poets, various twentieth-century writers, the ballet dancer Vaslav Nijinsky, and pop-culture references like Marilyn Monroe. They share the stage with a surreal retinue of hags, cannibals, enchanted animals, mysterious strangers ("the pilot" who appears in several poems, "the gentleman" in "The Hill"), life forms without a name ("Life"), and other nameless presences that find expression in geometric shapes or shadowed outlines.

On many occasions, when asked to explain his work, Šalamun would answer sincerely: "I describe what I see." Without going into the vastness of subjectivity that this suggests, Šalamun's poetic language is clearly and precisely visual. The mental imagery he creates (or recreates) through language is, however, by far more fluid and fantastic than what one could ever get away with in any visual art medium. Many of his poems could be read as shot-lists for the most fantastic avant-garde films that can never be made.

In the same way thoughts and dreams play themselves out across the "screen" of one's mind, so do many of Šalamun's poems in *Andes*, which, as mental projections through language, can sometimes seem to flicker in and out of view like pixilated holograms. Like dream language, Šalamun's language and the images it creates can be both familiar and otherworldly at the same time. Kaleidoscopic images, like so many cloud shapes, move through the pages of this book and like clouds are mutable, open to interpretation. All I know for certain is that, as translators, we heeded Šalamun's advice to stay literal. We tried to stay as faithful as possible to what Šalamun wrote *the way he wrote it.*

There were moments of untranslatability when we had to take certain liberties, which Šalamun encouraged and approved, but for the most part, whenever we strayed from the literal path, we would inevitably end up on a road to nowhere and had to retrace our steps back to the source, which is the line, the individual word or words, the mood, syntax, the sound, and rhythm—all these components of language that Šalamun works with the way a painter works with oil and brushstrokes or a stonecutter works with chisel and stone. Or the way medieval mystics worked with language to tap pigeons from walls, to create "something from nothing," as Šalamun once described to me in an interview, or as he writes in *Andes*'s first poem, "Among the Chestnuts", speaking of his "child": "I made him out of / shadows and firmed him with / halva."

Šalamun was aware how easy it is to say that his poetry "doesn't make sense" and often joked about this, including at public readings. He could sympathize with his critics, usually from Slovenia, that his lines could seem like those of madman, or as he once described it to me, in all sincerity, as something "preverbal, before language." He went on to label himself as "the only illiterate writer," which is quite a statement, considering how erudite and well read he was. But knowing that he never spoke with irony, he meant what he said: He also does not know what all this language is, where it comes from, or what it means. He only knows that *it is*, and that it is his nature to work with it, destroy it, reassemble it, fly with it and over it, and dive below. His goal was not to understand what he was doing but, as he explained to us: "To be the master of not-knowing."

In Šalamun, the message is the medium, and the medium is language, with its multiple layers of "meaning" like so many layers of sediment at the bottom of the sea. Much of *Andes* can perhaps be better "understood" not so much as meaning conveyed in words, but as mental energy transformed and *brought to life through language*. One of the many interesting things about Šalamun is how he is able to move through different levels of language and consciousness, like a radio dial scrolling through the frequencies of being, and decant all this vibrating energy into a language that, no matter how strange, can still resonate with other people.

To be sure, there are moments in *Andes* where Šalamun's relentless mix of mental manifestations, levels of language, and layers of references can be overwhelming, even for the poet himself. For example, in "Syracuse," Šalamun writes, "This is for MŠ." When I asked who this is, he replied, slightly embarrassed, "I don't remember." Or the reference in the poem "Hedgehog" to the "ostrich with gabon"—we quizzed him on this and he admitted, sheepishly, "Oh yes, that doesn't make any sense. But please leave it as it is." So there you go.

Contradiction, paradox, and non-comprehension are part and parcel of the Šalamunian universe, so it is no surprise that there were moments working together with him when I experienced all three simultaneously. One day, for example, he changed the title of the poem "Tigris, Čistina" in the original, which we had (I thought quite nicely) translated as "Tigris, Purity," to "Tigris Fioreto." When asked why, he just shrugged. When I asked if he would make the same change to the original, he answered, "No. Next question."

Šalamun saw no discrepancy in this, which at first frustrated me, but I learned over time that he saw the process of translation as a chance to recreate his poems in English. He knew that an exact, mirror copy of the original in another language was unachievable, and I don't think he ever concerned himself with what he could not do. He believed passionately that poetry could be reborn in translation, knowing how much gets lost when one tries to transfer a work of art made of words from one language to another. Šalamun was an optimist of the highest order. It is not what is lost in translation, but what is gained, that most interested him.

Because we discussed this together, I know Šalamun believed it possible for a translation to compensate, even if in a limited way, for what gets lost by discovering or creating something that is fresh, unexpected, or new—even (and usually) when this appears in another place inside the poem or even another poem inside the book. I know that wherever this happened in *Andes* (e.g., the neologism "steelily" in "White Greeks" is a translation of a real word in Slovenian), it made Šalamun happy, and he had no qualms about differences in language versions that this "energy transference" created. It is as if the energy of the original line, the original poem, is looking for the organic way in translation to express whatever it is that it expresses through the poet in the original text.

But what, in Šalamun's case, actually is the original? He once told me, during an interview for the film, that in many ways his Slovenian texts are themselves "translations" of the language that he experienced during the act of writing. The original is somehow poetry before language, or beyond language, or however you wish to visualize this thing that enters, embodies, and is reborn within a poet in the form of a poem—a form that seldom, if ever, can do justice to the inspiration that brought it into being. So in this sense, a translation into another language is twice removed from the original. It is an echo of an echo.

Happily, as I mentioned, Šalamun was an optimist. He believed that writing poetry was possible, regardless of what "gets lost" or changes (or gets misunderstood) in the act of writing it down. By extension, he believed in the ability to transfer the energy of poetry from one language to another, from one person to another, through the medium of poetry-in-translation. From interviews we did together, I know he believed in poetry's power to open spaces for people to understand themselves and the world around them. Šalamun's poetry is universal (and therefore universally translatable) because it speaks from, and for, our true nature as human beings.

Another thing I learned working with Šalamun on these poems is that much of what might seem strange to me or you, at least at first sight, was to him very matter-of-fact. Spending time with him, I began to realize that the way Šalamun wrote poetry was not so different from how he spoke, and probably very similar to the way he thought and dreamt. It was all one language to him. Poetry was how he spoke with the world. It was his life, his job, his lover, his friend, his teacher, and it was also at times his monster, his mirror, and his veil. As a poet, Šalamun was always and only himself. Through the language of his poetry, he was an indefatigable explorer of the inner workings and outer boundaries of his "self"—its polymorphous and boundless nature, and ultimately, its emptiness and non-existence.

Hegel, in one of his lectures on aesthetics, writes: "Poetry is the universal art of the mind that has become free in its own nature." I can't think of a better description of Šalamun's poetry and what it is that he is doing when he commits words to paper. Because it is "free in its own nature," Šalamun's poetry benefits from a gentle reading and also repeated reading. Like most of the best things in life, it is not possible to accurately describe the experience—one can only dive into it, headfirst, and let the words wash over you. As William Blake (referenced in *Andes*) wrote over two centuries ago—a line that could have come from Šalamun at any point during his long career: "Dip him in the river who loves water."

It is encouraging that, by my count, *Andes* is now the sixth complete book of Šalamun's translated and published in English as it was originally written. The others are: *A Ballad for Metka Krašovec* (2001), *Poker* (2003), *The Blue Tower* (2011), *On the Tracks of Wild Game (*2012), and *Soy Realidad* (2014). Reading Šalamun in book form is to encounter his art the way he intended it to be experienced. The poems that form *Andes* were written together, in a typical burst of Šalamunian energy, during one of his stays in Tuscany, at the Santa Maddelena writers' retreat— the same place, incidentally, where he wrote *The Blue Tower*— and in my opinion they are best appreciated when they are read together in a similar way.

I should also mention that the publication of *Andes* by Black Ocean marks the first time that a Šalamun manuscript is published in English before publication in Slovenian. I think this would tickle Tomaž. America, as he once wrote prophetically, is his destiny.

— *Jeffrey Young, Prague–Ljubljana, June 2016*

I

Sometimes Suzanne weeps a little and Jean-Michel says, "Shut up, Venus. I know what it is like to be tied up and fed, with a bowl of rice on the floor, like an animal. I once counted my bruises and I had 32!"

— Jennifer Clement, quoting Jean-Michel Basquiat

AMONG THE CHESTNUTS

I stepped on my broken finger on
the horse and ate a sweetie.
I raised and rounded my shoulders.
They called me Wilhelm von Tegetthoff,
who rolls in the dew.
Minka brought me *potica*.
She turned me into a broom.
I felt hands on the stove and under the stove.
In between was also feeding firewood.
That's how we lived in groves on
the second floor.
Friends visited me.
I watered the plants, which also my child
noticed. I made him out of
shadows and firmed him with
halva.
Pins stuck to him, pins.
And he became a great cavalier
in faraway lands on terraces.

CONCLUDING OF A SMALL BALL

A Latin sponge, soiled.
Rembrandt with a hard

key. Villages sing, villages.
The garden bed wavers.

O, light of stars, coloring itself,
we spread small socks.

Tufahija, you don't know what it is,
you'll learn, you'll learn,

now you're a grown-up. I rotate
the little diaper and throw you

out of it. As if I would have
sawdust in the head

and around it not skull
but crinkled paper.

I TOUCH ROUGH CANVAS ON THE DECK CHAIR

Would you stop the shovel as
it's loading? From

the bushes a poster
jumped and twirled

white iron. I pressed
its teeth with

jewels. The horse has
my breast,

I have the breast
of horses. Would

you stop the shovel as
it's loading?

I touch rough canvas on
the deck chair.

PLASMA, SMALL BREAD OF AVALA

As. This kind of complexion goes.
As this kind of complexion

dilates. Brown ones, small
buttery breads, drops don't

shatter. They burst.
The stalk is the basis

on the edge of a blue
butterfly. Traverses

the air. Lifts the wing. And
here I stepped into

the church of San Ivo della
Sapienza and

gave back to Borromini
the eye from the suitcase.

OSTRICH GALVANIZED WITH CYLINDER

One race is Mother's
small loaf.

I will have firewood. Vikica
Falls. C'mon

little fur.
Catfish done on green.

Figure on release. The grave,
which hollowed out

the spindle and left behind
nuts. Added

slalom. Gothic script. To roll up
the vest.

I twist beak as
crow twists its wire.

HE ACQUAINTED THE DEAD ONE WITH THE HABSBURGS

We go along the slope of the Potomac.
A measle's bill.

Game, wild game. Delta
hurts. Poppy blooms.

Kir, little needles. Bronze becomes
golden. Doe, put on your

little coat! Otto, open the doors!
The pea drizzles, the scythe drizzles,

on a boat a man wrests
from a wrist. Drags color,

throws diamond pretzel. Breath hurts.
Breath be brave.

With trees we filled in
long thin rectum.

HE EXCLAIMED

A cat creeps with
mouth movements,

not with shoes. We run and from
us flutter little tassels.

The paw goes into the wrap, into cylinder,
it gathers on the bottom

like water. Stars protrude.
Birds break branches.

The stars smack with open
mouths, I bumped into

wreathes of pearls. Thunder!
Shut the door! Draw

Tom Sawyer! May the Circassian
lie here, forever.

BREATH COMES FROM DISFIGURE

Are we a rowboat? Are we a rowboat?
Kara bloodshot, she-of-ours,

here, where I set you,
oars are mine, I eat your

eyes. Shrub, goofball, tact,
the world goes into two

with a shovel. Coat, kneel down coat,
your bones are hard, white

as yogurt, little ants scamper
over them undisturbed,

their lungs are spreading. I
looked at roots and the moon.

I looked at roots and the
moon. Shiva is dazed.

SHE HAD BLACK AND BEAUTIFUL EYES

Suzanne spills
pulp. On

the scale! On azure
bronze! We decide for

prey. Quinine. Quinine.
Quinine. Quinine

moistens the middle. He
held her under

the table. Sometimes he
pulled her out,

did sex with her,
shoved her back and

painted all the time. She had
black and beautiful eyes.

TO SPEED. TO THROW LAUNDRY INTO THE COFFIN

We warmed up small brown animals.
They were taming their little furs.

The ribbon's end lay in a black cave.
Busts were blocking it.

To find and to search and to boil and to spill,
as a little girl I was raped,

they were throwing me headfirst into the wall, I was
picking pears and fell from the ladder.

In the morning in the pool we found
a drowned man. Son wriggled out

from my hands like a weasel. I coated
the bell on the inner side

with plastic. We mumbled. With sketches
we operated on our teeth.

LUNCH AND THE EVENING

O, my virgin kleptomaniac. You're
stepping on lilies. You're aping divas,

with a tiny overcoat you cry. Kaput!
Kaput! The femur.

Yesterday I saw

a Korean woman.
She was wiggling her toes. And when

she was bowing, when she was
bowing. Yesterday

I lunched with Amir. I hugged
him. Yesterday I

sat in the fifth row. This is
the best row in

the world in the hall of Spanish Fighters
in Moste in Ljubljana.

TWO

The two of us in a building.
The two of us in the dark.

We two drink dew.
We two look at Buddha.

Koblar is iodine.
Zwitter is iodine.

Izo is iodine.
Cvit, not Zwitter.

I slept under the parasol.
Daisies devoured

me. Rivers are our
tendrils. Food,

piranha, they set out for you
already long ago.

A MOUSE GOT CAUGHT IN A POT IN KATORGA

Plaques of candied big
yellow pigs

pluck themselves from nature. Twigs
ail. The dry branch

ails. Plaques of candied
big yellow

swine have eyes. They swim in
the sun. Eyes. Are

sweet. Eyes. Eyes that
carry white whales

make a cone. Respectfully
and proudly. They don't

blink. They don't nibble.
They are in powder.

POEMS

The ostrich pries open the little house
and takes

out the palimpsest.
My little bird

sits still. Puts on
feathers.

Joshua's little bird is not
Joshua's, is

alone. Drinks nature,
does not

crumble. Looks
and does not

budge.
Is submerged.

AND UNDER THE SKULL BREATHES COSMÉ TURRA

Monkeys bury
monkeys. In Ferrara

they drag a cart. Quadriga,
Rambla, between fingers

night and cold. Lucio Dalla
is dying.

The Pope's armor will
melt. Marco

is crying. Monkeys bury
monkeys. In Ferrara

they drag a cart. The wheel
staggers from

happiness. And moss.
And pain and feet.

The Self, pure awareness, shines as the light within the heart, surrounded by the senses. Only seeming to think, seeming to move, the Self neither sleeps nor wakes nor dreams.

—Upanishads

UNDER GLASS AIR SPEWS

I walk. Under glass air spews.
I opened little belts. Rushes and
a small basket was woven already inside
water. After the fish went sludge. The water
was religious. Rhinos were lying in it
inside a matchbox. Were there
also Tokyo streets? When you fall into the cylinder, into
the silo, they intercept the corpse. With a net. With
hooks. By dragging. "Leg already
stiffened, neck not yet," goes into the report.
With one race like this, with another race like that.
In the soft sun a small white-eared rabbit hops along
mountain pastures. He darts with a skiff through the forest
over cranberries and heather and strengthens his spirit.

SHE SAID PROUDLY, NOT SHOUTED

Hostages from high school, whose
white knees stick out,

come out. Come out!
Where out? Here we lie,

here we move our legs. The kiosk
is closing. The shutters roll

down. I bet that my car would
get scuffed,

but it didn't. And the Apennines
are snowed in,

the exit ramp from the hotel was steep. The shrub
is thick. And Mrs.

Nardelli while on a visit shouted
I'm from Čepovan!

HEDGEHOG

They beat me
on the bier.

Brothers. And patricians,
who spilled Scout's soup

on themselves.
Religiously insane

they drank to the last cow.
Ostrich with gabon

rolls barrels and I
lean with

elbows on cones.
And when you fasten

a pancake, it enlightens you
as in a fairy tale.

GROTTO

That the little flames won't
lick me. Four of them with turbans,

four with beards. Here I stand
on the rubber floor,

in front of me, you, Gorki,
played billiards on

Capri. For Ron in
Venice I bought

a jacket. The two of us
cooled off. Thick are wasps,

clauses. Two headscarves. For God
and stamen.

The norm. Wind cuts. Nabucco.
Flame of the gobbling mouth.

TIGRIS FIORETO

After I had more times wrung-myself-loose-through-the-wringer,
a doe attacked me. She rolled white

timbers with ψ echo. Shakti, I said,
Shakti, are you bruised? The drawer

cut your little apron, closing
awkwardly. I wormed in under the

vine. Exactly that vine in Brda where I
lost my virginity. I there,

she on Pohorje. In Brda I was
weak. Next time better and true.

O, warming of stones! O girls, girls,
big clumsy girls. No, not from Koper, but the ones

of Petrarch from Spain. Whether yes. Whether
yonder. Whether there. On the head with a milk can.

HORSE DOESN'T BETRAY

Although I moved in pointers,
ehm, I gargled fluff. Although I rode

the mare, I fell. You said you are
unbearably bored. Go

naked on the horse. Lay yourself down on
a log. Put on linens.

Make corks wild. Eat up blueberries.
Tear soft branches. Do you

feel them? You grab, smell, show. Do you
shoot them? Don't kill Marilyn

Monroe. Fix a drink. March among
trout. Forget the horse and return

to him. The moon will still be in the
sky. Only in another corner.

DADO

Double? Are you caught in a mattress?
In a vanity lizards are lying

with disassembled legs. Bees
fly and expend themselves, the road

turns. This is a polyvinyl strongbox,
God is a polyvinyl strongbox in

the mouths of beauties. Pastures there the subjunctive,
hired as an observer. Sweet

word, peat between papers. I remember
how it gushed between Dado's

big toe and that other long
toe without a name,

standing on clay. Bulatović
brought him out of mercy.

RECONQUISTA

The school casts shadow onto the courtyard.
I appeared in high boots, even though it was
dry.
They were copies, but they had heart.
People thronged.
A wheel of fortune from cut felt in the shape of
ducks' legs.
From thighs and porcelain—hemlocks.
This is the six-hundredth lowland.
The violin gliding, the violin Eve.
Gaudeamus.
Mail wagon.
Fathers hidden behind thick leather.
I'll cut out dwarfs and lay them in ditches.
They will have a finding wheel and the bill
written in black coal on the wall of the Escorial.
Wives climb.
Silent buds turn whales.

WHIRL

The word NORMAL imprints itself
inside the crypt and frightens

Glagolitic priests. I open the wall.
I sit on

the grass. I lean against
the wall. White lumps of lye,

what do you want? My eyes are
safe. The wall is a

mogul's wall. No connection between a dolphin
in the air and a dolphin in

water. Those three drops are betrayal.
The moon *is not* a round pontoon,

it's not. It's not a piece of mantra in a little notebook.
I'm leaning on honey.

KNOW WHAT! I WANT!

Allowances are those tendrils that twist
around the Doric columns

of Cocteau's boxwood. Here I would also
be buried. Would look at the sea. Would

have a Polish noblewoman beside me. Was
she the aunt, mother, great-great aunt, and

great-great grandmother of Miłosz Biedrzycki?
She thundered with a little fur. Afterwards

they became desolate and crept with a wheelbarrow.
But not in her generation,

later. But Katka comes there. And marries
that kind. And again everything surfaces.

With Miłosz we tiptoe America.
And both of us smelt out by Bagrzelska.

THE RAVINE

Hints. Spies.
Zone B. Zone B. Zone B. Zone B.

Zone A.
Give the little beauty!

You the little beauty to me,
I, the drain, to you.

Blood at the neck.
Parachutists,

who want also to be at the same time
ballet dancers, kill

themselves.
We closed

the bridge's nose
with a clothespin.

HERMES WAS ABLE TO CHANGE THE SOLES OF EVERY SHOEMAKER

Once in Petrinje under a pile of
wood I saw Bibica, the friend of

Camille. Together they strolled around
Rodin's garden. Choose quickly!

Rodin's garden misleads. The test always
has a false, hidden key.

The first paws fall on the chin
instantly. They scratch themselves and

cease. The others say, now we are
here, only a few of us left, but we are

the elite. Only one will be chosen. This one
they then cook and eat.

They roll his handfuls around in the mouth,
that the memory doesn't get lost.

PTUJ

We pricked ourselves, somewhere along the way, but we don't
know where.
Where did swallows escape us?
Our bellies hang from trains.
Yesterday there were still
sparks falling into our eye, if we gazed
too much. Like a Tic Tac.
That's why he didn't go into the army.
He was cross-eyed too, when he was a freshman, and a fantastic
saxophone player, even Vladimir Lovec
remembered him from the bar.
He brought in fish from Trieste and then
ran off into the snow. It was hardest
on the Italian-Swiss border.
There they almost shot him, but then
he saw Aunt Ines. Her father's chimneys
were smoking, and when the old guy
said to him, this is
Poussin, he got married.
It wasn't Poussin and that leg was
grazed. He also said
jump! and I really did jump, to
Cilka's, Mother's, Grandmother's, and
Great-grandmother's horror. And we played rodeo on
glass potties with Katka.

BUY HIS HOUSE IN KAMBREŠKO

One step, polished rock.
Order.
If I drink and talk too much, the tuna
will leave the Kvarner Bay.
That's how they shot the Italians. Mamma!
thud! and he fell into the gorge.
As he was falling, he no longer screamed, because
the Italians were always scared.
In Persia those scavengers we called
pigeons. We cut our finger, that it ran
blood, that pigeons would see.
We're chopped meat.
Ramanujan fried his own father
so that the fat dripped.
First into the trench, then slowly into the Ganges.
And Primož, in the couchette below me,
swam through it with his tires.

ACCORDING TO THE RAFTSMAN'S FLOOR PLAN TO OPERATE ON BRAIN NUCLEUS

Suitors with discs, who are you?
Are you Henkel employees?

Do you all have tiny new coats? You stuffed
yourselves inside an ant hill with

little heads bent.
You bleed yourselves. Do you

get a snack for each day
of leaking? A warm meal,

before the train? To roll barrels of blood
into nightmare, to roll barrels of blood into

dawn. Barrels, wound with bricks and
plasticine travel like this:

native hill—Luče—the Savinja—
Sava—Danube—Black Sea.

SKULL BASE

The skull base spreads. There
it storms ham hock. Bathes it.

In a lake. In sediment. An eraser
or a more than three-

kilometer-long strip.
All this we do.

At the base sprang
flowers. We can

turn them around and plant
them again. We walk

on the lake
in snowshoes as long as

snowshoes don't sink. Night
deepens into sand.

BIG YELLOW BLIND WITH JAVA

Rhododendron, what waits for you!
Your tendon, god of numbers,

your tendon. Said crunches.
Drizzles queens' heads.

Voooo, voooo howls the deer.
Frogs fall into the soil.

A little girl draws on dawn.
A stone cry sleeps in the skiff.

Water lilies and bronze, with olives.
With harnessed horses.

Flies between two layers of eyes
burned me. Here and there again

some small hoop. Here and there again some
brook. And hatred.

WHO DOESN'T HIDE BEHIND THE ALTAR

You shuffle! You move legs
and shuffle! Your legs

shiver like teenagers and
basketball players. If a boa

coils up, can you also jump over it?
Lard feasts on the cylinder.

Greasy inner circle of half hat.
Do you follow yourself? Nature whistles and beats

the herds. We draw a wall. We glue
snakes to trees. I'm deaf.

In youth I held incorrect
opinions. I'm dying and

setting my bed on fire. It's creamy.
I'm eternal, death says.

NINO

Palms will flash. Little flowers
dry out. From Ponte dell'Accademia you will

fall like some kind of rag. *There* Mušič
asked a young Slovenian who

had studied painting in Venice.
Have you ever heard of Zoran

Mušič? A worm has a limited ear.
Eats, till it is able. Eyes extinguish.

I wrap the steak in paper. Don't press yourself
down. Khlebnikov: about fat geometry

on a brisk tree. With a measure we measure
the belt. You know? That I would be even more fixed

in the sun. That I would lean on the Ca' Pesaro
with the apex from our stairs.

VADYANYITI (FROM BEHIND)

Vadyanyiti, yadyanyiti, drizzle, the golden background, snow.
Floor lacework, dung-beetle unicorn, a faerie, fruit.

Vadyanyiti, yadyanyiti. The portrait on the board in the closet
is coming unglued. We, clay, we fall. Rum in

the scissors. Avoid. Smolder. Carver's
red roof. Movement. Inscriptions. On the way back

I was accompanied by an UDBA agent and he chimed with
    a bicycle. Did
we understand each other? I stepped through a black

hallway and called out among the bars. Come out!
I guaranteed! From the windows on Miklošič Street

prisoners babbled. Not like in Perugia, where they
were on us, students, spitting from behind their

bars. Water is blue. The golden background pleases. And
Granny, with a hand fan, will receive me.

WITH AIR

Shuts eyes and sees. Species of people and lizards
were put together with honey

from the one and only blaze of stars. I go
on knees, by the stairs. Slivers are

torches. Splash. Eyes, ear, legs are vents.
I saw a duck. It was jumping on

a board. A shoulder lifted itself slightly above
the surface. My shoulders. This

I didn't notice alone. God seethes. We'll
persevere for another three months and twelve

years. To smell into Semezdin's soul
as he walks down the street. If the

statue would turn, would his coat turn,
too? What fixes him? Love?

HYDROGEN, LIST OF BIRDS IN THE ASTRAKHAN PROVINCE

With lament, in a closed arrow. Virtue with
capillaries, I'll wall you in into the house.

Through lungs. Through numbers, through senses.
We're harrowed up. The soil is still folded.

The clump clears it. The clump bounces and wraps it.
It is height. It is carpet. Honors stars and pashas.

Cardigans come out alone, without little feet.
What is lined with soft boards.

A wheelbarrow (a brush) falls over.
To look left, to look right,

to look into the sun and to the west. There
horses are run wild and horses are turned.

They are laid into the bolt. Dawn drips.
Yes, to lay horses softly into the bolt.

Words look like dead prostitutes, twisted, thin:
my subjective opinion.

—Heather Tone, "Likenesses"

PINK CASE

White flour forces fluff.
Kuad um Gondini, throws snowballs.

They went. Ed Vein.
Bucket-hairs.

Es Em Oy.
Vanni goes across the lawn with forearms.

The rod is. Walls in.
The Mrs. buys.

The boxwood grows together with waves of ketman.
With the husks of curtains.

Under the legs. Pink.
Teva Rome.

To be outside the sky is wiping the head.
Teva.

ON THE OPEN SEA

It was crowded on deck and first we
tossed over the ones who ate turnip.

We had to flock together on principle.
Father stood.

Livestock were barefoot and sole-worn.
Masqueraders built small mounds.

Her nephew sold halva.
First he introduces her.

Emma, Emma of the Carpathians, kin of
Alice. *Lust is lust.*

And so and so and so eats lusakogen.
Mounds of Venuses ride on a pony.

The captain glows. Father purrs.
I nod doors, scenery.

FILIBERT THE FAIR

Filibert
the Fair

is bolted behind
the door, he plays

with toy trains. What are you up to
Filibert

the Fair, I knock and
knock.

But
he

does
not

re
ply.

FERRARA, FERRARA

A minimal jewelry box with white
glycerin, the whirl is wicked because

it is lined. In purgatory we throw
dullards into baskets, some are

clinging to willow branches with their fine hairs. This hurts.
Some save sweets. This hurts.

Some become newts. They bite themselves up into
the casing of irons. They hiss over white

sheets, the shirts' edges. Steam comes
out also from them. We push out animals.

Let them sit on the wreath and ponder
there. Let them turn

legs at the hips. He said to me that
his chest flashed.

THE STREAM

He trained himself. Waits, till
water comes to his throat and

jumps over. Yet! wets
the page. Yet! wets

the spiny shell. From a chestnut,
from a chestnut, not from

an animal. This. Folds
a small barrel. And smashes all

the Cyrillic floors and exchanges them with
Beatrice's mother,

an Armenian. Now I gaze at
Paolo Mancini, *un*

ritratto della famiglia Del Corte.
Live slanted, teach the night.

WHITE GREEKS

We are that fish that pants at dawn and
eats at rhythm.
Wraps turban round and
round around its silver strands.
A pilot walks down the road. I had
seen him before in the skiff. He sat on an enormous ant.
The ant with its enormous
head bumped against his bottom.
Was he hopping?
He wasn't.
How was it then able to bump?
This I made up.
This I steelily made up.

Psst, psst, went the young men in Mexico
in the darkness inviting me among trees and
I really would go if Metka wouldn't grab me
by the arm and say: eat!
Then we were
robbed. They carried my corpse in
a warped trunk,
which I experienced in childhood on
Sušak, when they carried
the corpse of that fatso who had

a restaurant in La Roche,
Indiana.
The name thundered down into darkness.
And then they still had to transfer him to
Srakane.

Penthesilea! How she swims!
How her little legs fly out from the pinery.

NIJINSKY AND I

Sea of power. Sea of power pleases.
My reason here is lace.
Nicht plows it with furrow.
Vaslav thickens.
Body, will it cope?
Hiking boots, will they clean themselves?
Cut themselves to pieces. Host themselves.
Because sooner or later, when
the clock strikes, I'll be carried
away.
(That they would, that they would, that they would
have brought you from the rocky spring!)
That I would shoot down the wagon and wet it,
write to him
the last chapter and say
lacrima.

And hoo hoo, into jugs.
Each one who is scared will be licked by
the oath. And bare
heel. And lark.
A diamond cart.

If someone thinks that you can't pierce
the bladder of a crocodile in Switzerland, they're wrong.
There even much sooner.
The choir members perform early.
Everything is perfectly organized.
And then you scream: the sandals are scratching over
the snow, don't you see?
But the choir members are peacefully eating eyelashes
and they don't even need to pretend.
They really don't see.

THE PUPIL

Along a rubbed-out log an ant
promenades in a scratched-out corner.
This I learned among
Pygmies. It was kindergarten there.

Then I arrived by canoe to
Papua Guinea. Children were
throwing buns into the air, streams of brown
colors were rushing.

Huwah! Huwah! screamed the bearers
and threw bodies at our
feet. They protected us. Didn't eat us,
because to them we stank.
They ate only their young grandmothers.

Then I was sentenced. Nobody
will convince me of its injustice. With
soup I decanted myself from prison. Put
myself together like cars put themselves together in
commercials and rode off.

To Ferrara. To my Renaissance city.
And for the Papuans I sank a telephone pole
into the ground. All my caps that they will
discover in the leaves will be pooped in.

Schopenhauer (slimmer than St. Augustine)
knows what he knows. I also know what I know.
How they carried the hills.
They stood on stilts.

But the young, the bright, will comb their
eyelashes and say: this is
a normal urban motif, neither guilty nor
hungry.

AJUSCO

Crowns hissed and
spun in the upper tube.

A small rabbit meditated with me,
a small rabbit. I grabbed

him and tucked him under my
belt. We started to

descend. The walls were
moist from moss. We came to

a black rock and waited like
two fishermen. It waited for us.

A hit with a truck. A bomb.
And gentle lifting. A meadow.

Crystal drizzle. To the rabbit
with kohlrabi in its mouth.

JOSEPH II

When Joseph II moved, that it
drizzled and slammed with doors,

nobody noticed this. In the tower
the soldiers sat like bumblebees

on capes. Kevin Powers
resists this. I don't like

these pearl little boxes that fall
from the table. I am for my

youth. I am for thunder.
Tie and bind. Learn

to kick out the legs and push
the swing. To preserve white tarp

for goldfinches.
The clover, which is fragrant.

FOREIGNERS

What should be soothing still stays in the cage.
To start with a grasshopper and pluck
its legs like a child.

Clones are hiccupping crumbs.
The spoke must be enormous.
The waterfall falls. We also have five fingers.

We scheme miters.
We're digging up the fool.
Beneath the earth lie the bones of pendulums.
Always damp, we shove soil into an enormous
belly, where I alone
didn't light up the torches.

Ščep dies.
The letters sank under.
What Michael Jacobs uncovers, I cannot.

Palazzo. My palazzo is sunken.
To draw a small board for bees,
they will use it in the maze.

When we whooshed past the trees,
halls opened inside ears.
O, small breads for the dead!

Trousers rip on pine,
sometimes they don't.
From a tooth I took

the movie theater and stepped toward
Omega.
Danielle Losman was in

the other booth. Chinese were
lying there all over the floor.
Even more foreigners were lying all over the floor.

Wet lights are in white curtains.
Beetles crawl over them.
And the locomotive puffs and disappears.

BREAKFAST WITH HIM

The tub is hot,
a beet swims inside it.

The sultan shuts his ears,
dives in.

A fish
split up my

ear, heart, and
belly.

I nibbled on cherries with
my eyes. Wrung

the corpse of Ramanujan's
father.

Still the fat dripped.
Into him.

GRAIN OF PRACTICES

To shift
hands in

life means
to move

rocks into
death.

To whistle
on small flags, which are

climbed around
or encircled by

ants. They are
metered feet.

They are backgammons
of the spirit.

TUFT PRESSES ME

Man
twists his

leg on a round
step.

Man falls
in love

with a round
head.

An idiot
generalizes,

Blake said
long ago.

With drama, because he had
my teeth.

INDIANS LITTLE JAPANESE

In the pool, among so many snow white
little Japanese, a black corpse was lying
below a neon light.

It didn't twitch, it didn't swim, I was
disquieted.
Then the corpse started to cackle and said that he is

a drummer, in Tokyo on a visit from Memphis.
But don't you have more like
country music there, I asked

and white and black are already now
rolling on the second floor under gentle
light.

All the way up young men were lying in sleeping
bags and looking at the stars.
I saw GPS for the first time.

I had no clue that Tokyo
taxi drivers have such small white gloves.
It wasn't *Enter the Void*.

Our hotel was next to the Emperor's palace.
Only at the full moon did I go to such places
in the middle of the night.

THE BLOSSOM FALLS, PEOPLE DIE

When I had read the book *Ghost Train*
Through the Andes by Michael
Jacobs and stepped before
the threshold
con mia ultima sigaretta
with a glass of wine
I quietly called inside myself
Sophie! Sophie!
how he revived you, how you are present
today, here inside me.
I admire you!

And it's about Michael Jacob's grandmother, he lives in
Spain with a beautiful dog,
travels all his life and writes beautiful books.
And he defended Blunt, publically,
Blunt according to him was not an active spy from
the war onward, the Queen
forgave him.
Michael, Waheed, Alex, and Beatrice now
happily babble, I look at
stars,
quietly calling Sophie.

TUSCANY

In the evening, when the caterpillar swaddled an infant and its
shadow . . . don't lean on the peach blossom! don't

lean on the peach blossom! at most on the trunk with
your back, so in the evening, when the caterpillar swaddled

an infant and its shadow, the machine moved away
an inch. Lit up a chest full of watercraft. Our corn

got paralyzed. Our apples got paralyzed.
Boxes don't shut anymore. The city

moved away. Drawbridges rotted and fell into
the water. Look Mrs. Nerina. Now I will

spark a match and burn down your eyebrows. You will sing with
a feeble voice and, what's more, through glass. We drove

on the road of the Seven Bridges. Above us were
brown anthills, below us silver streams.

FIRST AFRICA

Kings are anchors.
Queens are anchorages.
Osmosis is a white canvas, you won't
believe it.

And Hannibal, a man of distinction, who was swung by
twilight on fat elephants, he didn't allow himself
to be overcome. Was he baked from wild game,
was wild game baked out from them?

One happy browne one,
one happy green one,
one happy spring one,
one happy iron one.

In Kenya the butcher rules, he chopped our
little belly and inside found:
forks, a knife, a ring from the meat of another body and
a musical instrument.

Jackals shout, lock him up!

But we swore to him.

THE CROUCHING ONES ARE DRAWING NEAR THEM

Io me ne vado, coniglio,
I'm leaving you.

The little ball is wooden. Like motion. Like
motion. Like motion,

she got entangled. Hatch a shovel.
Hide silence in the breast.

Enstrengthen her, enstrengthen her.
Will she start to boil? Parked

under a Renaissance garage, later
under a lily. Horses will

find affection for flies. They
won't twitch anymore with

eyelids and crystals. The crouching ones
are drawing near them.

BELOVED METKA

Beloved Metka, how is it that
the self doesn't allow you to
your self? That you torture and torture yourself like a wounded and
betrayed animal in a cage, bleeding at the
bars, inflicting yourself with deep, even
deeper wounds.
How is it that my love cannot
help you. I am your
husband, your beloved, I was your
midwife at your
paintings, your source of ache and
longing, why do you go so
far? Don't you think that you go
too far?

Don't dry yourself out.

Don't spin in a circle like a blind animal,
stiff from fear, lapping sorrow.
Please don't roll these dreadful rocks of dusk
onto yourself or anyone else. Everything is within
reach of reason and arms and heart and spring and
rain and river, in which you swim in
Brazil among friends.
That is why I gave you

the Upanishads and asked you to read them
every day. I hope that you do.
I hope that the swimming will
soften you, wash you, smooth you,
liberate you.

And don't forget, this is from
long ago. Nikita Stanescu, when he saw you for the first
time, said, *La douleur qui marche*
and kissed your hand.

I ask you, please, unburden yourself.

TURN

When Hermes, crouched, emptied the turtle,
crumbs dripped out of his
mouth.
From crumbs he made Greta Garbo
a bridge.
He bought her a scarf.
Once he hung her by the legs.
Greta Garbo was only a
bit more talented than
Ita Rina.
Greta Garbo has nothing. Like
Jackie she sometimes snuck
into MOMA by the side door and looked
at something, but only as long as she was
alive.
Kynaston and Drenka were
let go. Both were saved
by the love of the world,
us, brothers and sisters,
uncles and nephews and sons and
fathers and paws on the shoulder and into the mountains,
we are in Japan.
There let me be slightly snowed in.

One old woman gently rests, the other rolls
from the mountain—felling trees, rocks
bouncing her—into my dream. There
splashes.
Old women have their
asses propped up by spruce and beams.
They cook people, boil them up and
kick.
They throw discs, eyes shut.
And glue heads into albums.

IV

For example, we know that Wittgenstein (Ludwig)
  is in paradise.
Also, that the body can neither be described nor shown.

—Arkady Dragomoshchenko

CHIPPED STEPS OF PAOLO MANCINI

There will be war. We will ride with kachugas over these
waters around the hill. The pyramids will
open. Small black men with shovels
will stand at the entrances.
Come, come, kind souls will
nod, we will protect you.
Here we have torches. Tarot cards. A live
monkey, which Velazquez was painting.
A folio of publications and rivers and
waterfalls.

And we are the most proud of
Paolo Mancini, who abolished the death
penalty. With a pair of compasses he pierced the papal
head and established oases. They tore his
skin off down to the ribs and left it at
the legs. Today only James
Powderly licks these frescoes. With a team. With
torches that illuminate him.

Only the Persians correctly interpreted
the canisters. They were bounced back at the front.
Then they started to soften in
fleece and pull back. They pitched their
tents and soaped up. There weren't
enough oars. They stole them for themselves on boats with torn
leather. The bronze of forks shines and faints.
The little cart runs.

WE WON'T ARGUE OVER ONE WORKER

He gave off strange signals when he
washed. He had a chest like a
picador.

I got human
fins and a small bottle of
pearls.

Mules were on the rooftops
doing their laundry.
Prayer mills rattling,
trucks rushing down
the streets.

*No vamos pelear por un
obrero*, my housekeeper
said. He was shot by
mistake, by Camacho, standing behind
cases.

GIOVENTU UNIVERSITARIA FASCISTA

Mai, mai, moves the head and moon.
A half-baked word is the one most
eaten. Slides down.
Glues itself to the sky. Do they till with the plow also through
a live body as through some
volcano?

I remember that it hissed at the crater.
That they were calming me.
So it hisses in peace already for two thousand years.
I didn't believe them.
I was very vain and arbitrary,
but always totally adequate
for the homeland. Because the volcano
lifted up.

Butchered houses and trees and handles and
beasts on the windows. Tacitus barely saved himself and
set sail, not Tacitus, Pliny.
Pirandello and Malaparte observed all of this from the
terrace and waved to Axel Munthe.

Do you see? Do you see? The sea
boiled over.
To the young girl Fascists they distributed
small goji balls, that they would be vigorous and that they would
grow and that they would approve a stipendium
for my mother.

LIFE

That thorns would be sprinkled with mushrooms.
That they would find lice in turbans when they would iron
them. That they would all enclose themselves in glass, old
    and young and together
honk at icicles.
Tito steps onto a blue
train. Takes his leave. In one container is
jam, in the other container is
hair. He carries his leg on the shoulder in
džulbastija.
He opens farmers' mouths with Archimedean
devices, that their little heart
jumps, breaks its own frames
and bleeds out.

All of us would like to give you life if we could
awaken you, Father. Look at this soil on my
knees. I drank the infusion and covered
myself with soil.
Puffed my breath into small flowers.
But one clumsy gendarme, whose leg
sank in, knocked out my right eye with his
heel. My arms were blocked
by weight and I couldn't

shove it back into the socket. It flew away. Like
the drink Nabokov refused on the hotel terrace in
Montreux.

Under glass chewing its lemon was a tiny white
ball. Life surrounded it with
stalagmites.

JOSEPH WRAPPED MARY INTO THICKLY WOVEN CANVAS

Shai, wrap, wrap, shai.
Shaddai El Shai.
Do not disfigure the face.
Look at it long.
Tap it, like Japanese women do to
rid themselves of wrinkles.

You do it like this: hillock, small hill, small hill, only
round *accents circonflexes*,
while I withstand the level field,
the openness without confusions and
the love.

To gaze long into a pool of eyes
and as Najla said.
These are the clearest
black eyes that I have seen in my
life.

We two are one.
We two are married.

That trip of ours to Pontassieve was the best.
Beautiful girls bathed us
and buzzed with their gadgets around
our ears and fine hairs.

BROTHER WHO FALLS ON BROTHER AS IF THEY WERE FROM THE SAME OVEN

So will you ever see
your face in boiling

liquid molasses? What you
wrote, you wrote, and now

I wrap it.
The seals

are opening, we're wounding
humanity.

I would sit on a sheet metal
windowsill,

look into the sun. The Vltava
was

shimmering. I left
naked to the waist.

THROWING THE BICYCLE OVER THE FENCE

Her, you-see-her-like-this, by placing
your arm underwater a few

inches, staring at your palm and then
you picture a fence,

over which in time a traveller throws
a bicycle,

because the fence disturbs him. He cannot
continue his way, he has no chance

of any guarantee that by this
throwing of the bicycle over

the fence, it won't break or
get damaged, but her, you-see-her-like-this,

you see. You hope and you hope that she won't be
too vexed.

SYRACUSE

He was alive. He was like a young hen and
newborn that cries softly.
The neighbors rumbled over
the stairs. With heavy shoes,
with fluff.

Not here, not here, this is for MŠ,
come here.

It was such a space, triangular,
painted gray-blue.

My farewell.
And doctorate and *shahid* and already then
flashes. And a shaver and small scissors.

To take reason.
To rush off on the bike and
destroy. To destroy.

MAIL TO AUSTIN

I sent you a package for
cleaning tiny ears. I don't care

about publications. Najla can
dig herself into a hill.

Don't smear footsteps
and shrieks. All, all,

he was thinking and
painted, portrayed trains and

his mother, showed
how he wakes up and

how he would like to escape, but still
before write an Iliad, about

himself, about Mother, about brothers, about
winter, about Winnipeg.

WE WILL TEAR YOUR THROAT
WITH BLUEBERRIES

Look, Piarist. In this little gray glove your
finger got wet. Hips rustled.
Čedo, moje milo čedo, we heard

shepherds and gods compete each with
their own stick. And some brought agaves, lyres,
an azure bird, delft plates, laurel and

hunting dogs. Who edits *Vogue*? Do you remember
how those two women crawled with their suitcases and
porters into George V? Here we have

groves. Plenty of space. All
the hidden nooks from history's climates.
Newts, shepherds, and Alices,

a famous she-dog, buried with my
ancestors not far from Griša's pyramid. Heroes groan.

Heroines groan. This still waits for us
both. Small gray and green hats. Moments
when we introduce ourselves and extend

hands. On the piazza. Here a weary farmer
brought grain into my granary. Cordially I
pet women and animals.

WE FROM ARAGON

When Vegeta cubes curl up inside the belly,
we can expect crisscross,
Vegeta posture, again some digging up of

a wall. Gelli will step out of his *Loggia P
due*, retract what was heaped
upon him and we will all get dewy little drops

in our eyes. We rip up thigh. We undress
the best skins for chandeliers. Then, when the most
famous veterinarian in the world

"I sewed back the upper part of the beak,
perforated it with supports and the photo
of my saved goose went around the world." Michael Jacobs,

a close friend of the editor of *The Observer*
(he personally asked that he bring him something
fresh from Italy), will now reshape this

into a story. Then we drove off with
jeeps along small steep paths and stepped into
the palace. Its name is bronze, gold, coffee.

DAUGHTER DREW IN ALSO THE HERBARIUM

I know, you lie on the back and say, here
fern, here blackberry and

waves start to twist, birds
quarrel and shriek from

pure oil and happiness and we,
Aragonese, who swore loyalty

to the king if he would defend us, if not,
not, *nos contra todos, todos contra*

nos, now we are both placed
each in his own end,

in front of the engraved inscription Tristan and
Isolde. For a few years they had a restaurant

here. We came for the ambiance
along hidden paths.

MORNING

Immortality comes and goes, don't blind yourself
young man. If you don't grab it by

the horns, it will look. At the moon. At a theodolite.
It will shine only on your coupled

brain, coupled heart, coupled T-shirt,
coupled eyes. Everything on you will be

edged, pressed, and crumpled. Hide
yourself under the snow and rest. In the storm,

when I had to release a barrel of oil into the sea
that it made an eye, a radiant barrel,

immortality hugged you. May it not be
the last time. Dante does not report on this. Neither

Ariosto, nor Torquato Tasso. Hold
yourself by the sleeves and fly away. Stay.

HOOPS

The horse got fed up with corks. It dashed,
laid, and foamed. Under the gallows

I rode death. My hip got
burned by heating.

Everything was of iron. Helmets, swords,
spurs, immense hoops

for tying on Palazzo
Strozzi. And a ghost. And

camels. And rust. And weeee, weeee
hissing. You have

guttural fingers. In the middle of the desert you draw
flowers. Some kneeled. Some

just watched. Some kneeled and
watched. Both of us.

YOU CRY BECAUSE MY LOVE ISN'T DEEPER, I KNOW

From Florence come plans, sketches,
deliberations and reasonings.

We don't give a damn about that. *Sono un
Slavo Dalmata*, a son of Venice.

Like Titian I fly from one to
another among colors. Like

Tiepolo we are both stretched by blueness. Joshua
says: we met by chance,

I don't know by which logic, in the basement of the Empire
State Building. Tomaž otherwise

had a total sense for algae. Only
money he didn't have and neither did I.

Now they sail above the country. Like some kind of dots.
Like some kind of dots, and I am jealous.

Each term may be traced back to its beginning as unity in the Monad, which itself arose from the incomprehensible mystery of zero.

—Michael S. Schneider,
A Beginner's Guide to Constructing the Universe

FROM STONE

I pushed him deeper into the slope.
The water was sweet and

tepid. For centuries the winch
hasn't worked.

Sing-alongs go to dust.
Scent is powder.

Algae, handled, harnessed
first into waves,

then into shudder. Shudder, shudder,
shudder on the shore. On the

shore by the boat. When the
drum, the ring around the

the cosmos, melts. We're inside a small house.
There's a fingerbreadth of the Lord.

POURING

Najdihojca was at first a corpse in
the hall to whom no one had yet given
birth.

Brothers-in-law rolled in
dough and jingled. We fixed small
pieces of blue glass into

fences. Did you prick yourself, or rather,
wound yourself? I have
bleeding hands.

The blood drips from
glass onto my
trousers.

My blood is lazy. My blood doesn't
climb. My blood wipes its
eyes with acacia.

Who writes out this order form? With
the last, last
rays. With

small silver beaks on
high steps. I will pour
over your hair.

THE FOREST

Ribbons stained themselves.
Mistakes died.
My azure son, my son.
I wait.
It is heated.
The balloon rises.
Veins, fields, snakes, spruce.
Dumpled bridges, beneath them Košice.
Gypsies with refrigerators and wings.
They open doors, they tear doors down.
Asters harnessed horses.
Water hurts.
The continent surfaces.
South America, northern shoes, dear to me.
Harvest-women.
Penthesileas.
A dog grubs through canals, bites lilies.
The whisper from the trees and rooftops.
Flashes of brown canvasses.
Complicitly you push aside the curtains,
you see?
Salty, where are so many gazelles, so many
nailed fish, tiles, all silver, wild,
alive.

A mini cone.

Beetroot and axe.

Now a newt, now a commons, arms, which swim in
a circle.

MONEY SHOTS

Do you love splendor, Sviščaki?
How to crawl out from the coat and dark spots to
the stream.
To Bronzino's chin, to his
lips. His forehead, to
the triptych.
Pellicole!
With a cancelled background, with white dogs.
Sheep-breeding drops.
The reed is cold.
Into you, into you, you cover up and recollect.
You call out to hills, so that they soften.
You bind the Savinja.
What with rags and brushes?
You're leaving me?
Which is not bush.
Which is not boxwood.
Is not only for the two of us.
Is not a barrel that you can exchange for eyes or
a grebe on the wall?

Did he start? Did he start? Did he unbutton?
Gattamelata, from column to column, from sidewalk to
pavement.

Everything is self-fulfilled. The Moskvitch gilds itself.
Blots ceremonies.
Disfigures and stuffs animals.
Sharpens. Sharpens.
Kisses crowns and sequences and looks from
the bus.
Rolls shards.
Changes tufts.
Lifts tiles with the back, with its brown
back. Doesn't see the blind one
anymore. Doesn't plough the blade.
My Tehran. My
thumbtack.
My dry abyss.
When I heat myself up. When I put myself on exhibition,
that the stars see me.
I cry you.

Dripping with white and yellow
flour.
What did auntie dream, how they
opened her skull?
How she exchanged chairs and
thread.
Blurry eyes.
From the theater.
I borrowed her from the theater.
There wasn't a tent camp and you turned yourself in.

I reached, I reached with the right hand and inserted a piece
of white paper into your small, membranous box where wolves
bud.

The most given.

The most given to tear the belly.

To show to monkeys spleen and the spirit of the great.

To tackle.

To side with the solvent.

To crumble with the rollercoaster.

And finally in front of the chain.

To take down.

To hear the wild screams of companions of animals of dogs.

Ivory meadows, inside them rolled

wires and mess tins and moss, with which they

washed the mess tins, the moss was taken out from

the stream. And spears caught fire,

they called over the skin.

Pickpockets nodded.

Here is the signboard, here is the signboard, they shouted,

shoemakers, not that they would be

aware.

And over rounded stones as with all

nations that translated the Bible

too late.

The graft will rot.

With the sixth brigade, with big shoes, with
a pot on the back.
With a nun, stripped, blissfully blown out and
pacified.
Columbus drinks.
Šamici štrafaniči, who wanted and bound you.
Sent and turned over.
Accommodated with mirrors.

My warrior. My raver. My happiness. My
tunnel. Benches placed flat into
Sanskrit. We two devour posters.
We two glide a small ball.
We two look for a billfold and find it.
You touch the turtle.
I touch the turtle under the roof and Kamila.
Where small flowers grow.
Where with sun and scourge
we roll. We roll what
we roll.

Sequoia prepare spruce.
The sun germinates inside us both behind bars and in front of bars.
The peacock, did it dress up in a man's corpse?
Didn't it see?
Did it plant a brick-colored brick and
doorman with pride?
Dripped, dripped, meowingly wounded

the sack to its pleasure.
Rubbed down hearing and sweat.

Moneyshots.
Each one was sated by Fra Angelico.

THE CELL

I joy. It's good to be. I'm the rattle
of order. With ossicle

of eye I fumble into the bathtub.
The tower's witness vomits

blood. Fra Angelico pours
over all monks. I tasted

you. We live as
we live. My legs

jut out, from the calmed
crane. At least over there.

At least over there. At least over here. The ferry
has pixie eyes.

DAVID SCHUBERT

I tore the cap from my cheek, put it to
my ear and spoke, this is a microphone, a frog with
a mouth. A drop of clay, the remains of the shepherd.
To mess the bridge? To mess up the bone? To truly once
break through to there. There, where darkness is. Where
no foxes are. Foxes were here only once,
sniffing something, they headed over the mountain and went
to Tibet to get Gilgamesh. Their grannies
wove out machines and were throwing them into boiling
fat. In between, in the heart of the grove, a boxwood grew.
And there in the circle slept David
Schubert, who wandered around the country with
the sun, with a paper bag in bread. It could
no longer be adjusted, not even with a monkey wrench.

TOMILE!

Not bird, not smoke, not chimney. It's a black
stain. The sun has not yet risen, or
we don't know that, because it's about the sketch, not about
nature. So will I dance into purgatory? So should I
hide behind the board, asks
the first female performer in the sketch. I turn the house
with a thrust, as if it were a spinning top, such that all
the furniture digs in into the walls and
falls onto the floor.
Boon, a boon, we discovered a well!
There, where before was the foundation, is
now a well. Later the other
inhabitant leans a book against the washboard,
neither agitated nor
disturbed. He likes to sunbathe. When he places the book on
the washboard, he does it with the thought that he will
sunbathe. There's no sun. It's a sketch.
The well vomits water like some kind of spring.

BLOCKED SYMMETRY

Someone threw off the axe as if the axe would bother
him. I throw it off, that my
fingers won't get glued to it.
If it is not yet buried and lies on
the sand, let it be buried. Let it drown,
let it rock away deeper. Alongside is
a pail. The population has not yet
woken up. Alongside are tufts of blue violets.
Alongside are weeds. Behind is
the sea. Baltic. Kristina and I
walked together on a wooden pier. Behind are
clouds and shtuza for the laundry. Shtuza: Lithuanian.
Rope. The grasses are pressed down.
High grasses are pressed down. The animal
is missing.

THE HILL

Šečerko, sugar-pie, I call the rabbit that I
tamed. Those naked branches, left of
the house, what kind of sense do they have?
Murmurs the chestnut.
Falling.
The chestnut is falling onto a helm.
Here is the cistern.
Here are dry leaves.
A corpse lies arced.
Vinedressers were licking their hands and fingers and
     encouraged each
other. Stuffed everything sweet.
Nodded.
On all fours they crawled off into
the hill and looked through the window at the gentleman who
     was eating.
The gentleman eats.
The gentleman places the spoon down onto an ox bone saucer.
Steps onto the balcony and shouts,
disgrace! disgrace! this piece is from ox.
You are logs.
You are stacked.
I saw nothing.

MARTYRDOM

I banged into the small room. People were fastened with
blue ribbons. A pelican was wounding its
young.
Eucalyptus.
Night.
The wind moves the eucalyptus leaves.
Tomorrow will be day.
It was that silverware that didn't
spill. Martyrdom electricity on small carts,
which were already used by the Phoenicians.
Me to unburden the corpse.
Also the other cried out the same.
Me to unburden the corpse.
This pushed in to the depth of the heart.
We became Levantines.
Turks washed out our dock and dust.

Donnini, March–April 2012

AFTERWORD: GHOSTWRITING THROUGH THE ANDES

A quick glimpse at the final shapeshifts of Tomaž Šalamun

Tibor Hrs Pandur

I am pure spirit,
without consequences.
—Šalamun: *The history of heaven is massive*[1]

Milton produced Paradise Lost in the way that a silkworm
produces silk, as the expression of his own nature.
—Karl Marx: *Theories of Surplus Value*

Andes is the penultimate authorized manuscript of Tomaž Šalamun. It is safe to claim that it is his most potent book since *The Blue Tower*. It presents us with a closing fractal of Šalamun's unconscious autobiography, an unprecedented poetic quest spanning multiple continents, peoples, states and histories.

Andes are hard to reach. Difficult to enter. The Slovene poet Miklavž Komelj said in his eulogy to Tomaž on January 5, 2015: "If today anyone is dead, it is certainly not Tomaž Šalamun, the immortal, eternal, bright Tomaž Šalamun, who wrote that he is leaving with his life to where he is, and that death was named mistakenly by those to whom the light

---

[1] From the book *Praznik (Feast)*, 1976 (translation mine).

was hidden. . . . .Tomaž Šalamun achieved this highest level, where the *real* question regarding his poetry isn't what someone thinks of it, or if someone likes it or not, but solely *if we are able to endure it or not.*" To endure the risk and danger of letting language run wherever it may, whatever it may brutally disclose.

Orgies, Babies, Breath, Molusk are the titles of his last published books in Slovenia. They all echo a quietude, a serene detachment ghostwritten in the wind. Words twinkle on the page and no one knows what they are, a dream prescribed is the closest I can get to describing them; words come into being without reason or regret as indefinable star-flakes, sparks of matter, unknowable fragments flickering in the dark like a memory about to be lost.

In the movie *Enter the Void* (explicitly referred to in *Andes*) the protagonist is killed at the beginning and floats above Tokyo (in bird's-eye view) as a bodiless spirit, a silent witness through whose eyes we witness the sad and brutal neon carnival of 21st century man. It is a movie that Tomaž described as a "shocking depiction of the human-condition." His recent poems are uttered in a similar vein as if by an ethereal ghost vaguely connected to his mortal coil, floating through the sad proceedings of this world, mixing personal memory with the public record, while retaining his visceral precision, transgressing occasionally into serene emphatic babble as if depicting the failure of language to present an infinitely complex multiverse, the absurdity of its potential inconsequentiality and its ultimate celebration in the face of the mortality of even memory itself.

The theme of death spreads through *Andes* in melancholic fractals, a slow face off into the void, to fall asleep, to enter beyond. The word "corpse" repeats the most throughout the book: corpses rise from the dead laughing, are being cooked, transported onto wagons and unloaded, to the point where Šalamun explicitly dreams his own passing ("White Greeks"), also in this formulation: "Under the gallows // I rode death." ("Hoops"). Death is ever-present. Death is borne, constantly faced in Šalamun. In *Andes*, it is, above all, a refusal to die, to stop production: "I am for my // youth. I am for thunder." ("Joseph II").

In many of his earlier poems, which take the form of epitaphs and parodic testaments, he writes as if already dead, musing on his own post-human condition: "at first I thought everything will be / clear and dandy after my death but that won't happen. Everyone / will stuff their heads with whatever they please / and then run around with this whatever causing even / greater confusion. who I've been and what it was I was / really doing no one will ever know."[2]

Šalamun's writing is generally characterized by a jovial spirit or ecstatic hedonism, a cheerful lightness with subversive trolling even, and above all, in the face of death.

When I first encountered Šalamun's poems they gave me a license to speak, that you are free to grant yourself the license to speak about anything in any way you choose. Šalamun is able (when at his best) to directly transmit the impulse to create without holding anything back. He wrote somewhere: "Whoever

---

2   Tomaž Šalamun: "The Visit, VI" from *On the Track of Wild Game*, 2012, Ugly Duckling Presse (translated by Sonja Kravanja).

doesn't step into the void, is an enemy of the people." His poetry by example gives you the impulse to step into the void. To share whatever is perceived as prohibited to share.

Šalamun is a language of his own, a multiplicity of tactics in a self-proclaimed experiment "of widening the spaces of freedom." He seems indecipherable by design, a language recycling machine, a constantly shifting topological map, with certain fixed nodes, orbiting around several crucial themes.

Because of his carnivalesque manner and multiple referred contexts, Šalamun has baffled literary historians searching for fixed meaning and resisted interpretation ever since. In other words: it is proverbially difficult to catch Šalamun with his pants down, because he always worked with his pants down already.

The Šalamun I most identified with is the early ecstatic, self-revealing, self-mythologizing, and myth-subverting Šalamun that breaks all internal, social, and linguistic conventions of censorship (openly professing his affairs with men while being married, revealing his dreams, obsessions, and transgressions), a tactic of brutal over-identification and re-appropriation on the battle front of the liberation of language. Using his "life" as material to be freely exploited in words, confessed, disclosed. That was his gamble; that was his play. And he went all the way.

In Šalamun the I is All. In all its simultaneous ambiguity. I would even venture to claim that most of Šalamun's poems can be seen as dream-texts: discharges of bodily surplus. Internal reports, private memories made public. Dreams captured on a verbal carrier, snatched from repression, written against oblivion. The poem (in the instance of dream-text) becomes a report on the struggle of consciousness to record unconscious mechanisms, while distorting and interpreting them with the very act of writing.

One of his famous definitions of poetry is: "Poetry, like beauty and / technology, is a field of perfect liberation / of all forces in a void."[3] Writing is revealed as a struggle to record oblivion and simultaneously as total "liberation of all forces" into oblivion. Šalamun's poetic method seems close to something Heiner Müller hoped to achieve: "The entire effort of writing consists in achieving the quality of one's own dreams, also the independence from interpretation."[4] Šalamun's shapeshift logic (the constant switching of positions from where he speaks) and the annulment of causal connections can be seen as reports of a dreaming mind. As Jung writes in *General Aspects of Dream Psychology*: "A dream is a theater in which the dreamer is himself the scene, the player, the prompter, the producer, the author, the public, and the critic." This method of switching among multiple, seemingly omnipresent narrators befits the simultaneity (or dispersal of difference) between object and subject in Šalamun's writing, the basic, complete unpredictability and uniqueness of every poem, structured in relation to other poems, clusters of nodes networking into space, linking in all directions. But although he is constantly switching modes, behind these masks he always

---

3   Tomaž Šalamun: "The Stage of the Manicheans" in *The Four Questions of Melancholy*, 1997, White Pine Press (translated by Michael Biggins).

4   Heiner Müller: *Krieg ohne Schlacht: Leben in zwei Diktaturen*, 2009, KiWi-Taschenbuch (translation mine).

remains himself. It is always Šalamun who speaks, constantly reaffirming his position, the very possibility of such writing, an endless conservation of memory of the very act of writing itself, referred to in "Hermes Was Able to Change the Soles of Every Shoemaker."

Šalamun seems to mimic a "pre-Cartesian alchemy where all is possible" as the Montenegrin poet Vladimir Ðurišić claims, or preconscious states of mind where no difference is perceived between objects, bodies, etc. Whatever I name, whatever I touch, I become, I am. As I speak I migrate souls and can become all there is: a flower, a clerical dignitary, a comet, brother, wife, lover, all I dream of, all I name, all I influence and am influenced by. This Šalamunian pantheism (arguing a child-like innocence faced with a world beyond human cognition), which simultaneously serves as justification for his transgressions, is still present in *Andes*. But if everything is one, if everything made from the same matter mates, devours, kills, and re-bears one another in endless cycles and then returns into space from which it is born again, then everything is permitted, all crime is innocence. At least in language. The Slovene literary critic Taras Kermauner tried to defend Šalamun in the 1980s and argued that it is not simple randomness of unreflected speech on Šalamun's part. For, if all is one, then all is potentially mine to use and misuse without accountability. Nothing matters and anything goes. For Šalamun there is no sin in language. In the grand scheme of things, all experience is seen as sacred and necessary. It seems that the entire effort of his writing is the conservation and constant affirmation of his right to say anything or whatever at all beyond consequence.

The man, who divined himself ("I am God and man in one"[5]), and strove to disperse himself into all there is (through and in language), speaks in *Andes* from the most vulnerable of species: "A worm has a limited ear. / Eats, till it is able. Eyes extinguish." ("Nino")
In *Andes* "breath hurts," but is kept steady. Shakti and Venus are bruised. Pain repeats. Everything aches. Especially women. And people in general. Grandmothers in dream fragments cook machines or are being cooked by people on strange expeditions; conquistadors, Indian autodidacts, generals, kings, and fascist dissident geniuses intermingle with Renaissance poets and architects—tragedies of journeys undertaken from books, solely in language, from one's own bed. Confined to dream as the only escape.

Words, organic matter, coded into an unpredictable neural network of future readings as "crystal drizzle," drizzling matter, cryptic dreamy pastures revealing/hiding unknowable mechanisms of the formation of language, passing scenes each as inconsequential or equally important as the next, an infinite boredom of endless becoming or entropy taking over the previously ecstatic syntrophic vigor and direct subversion; "dewy little drops"—inconsequential sad facts tangled in a dream of life fading into anecdotes or the impossibility of genuine communication, although glimpsed and celebrated as undeniable facts, micro-utopias of lovers and friends.

---

5   Tomaž Šalamun: "The Fish" in *The Four Questions of Melancholy*, 1997, White Pine Press (translated by Michael Biggins).

Despite all of these heavy sexualized dreamscapes of nostalgia, regret, lament, and rebellion, Šalamun retains immense awe and pleasure at the direct experience of the entire human organism; of the acceptance of violence as the currency of the world.[6] A celebration of eating while being eaten alive / by life[7]. Of being food, of being consumed by being. In the poem "Cell" he claims: "I joy. It's good to be."

The only thing that isn't dying in *Andes* is sex. Even the moment of death is clearly depicted as an act of release, a liberation of forces: "The name thundered down into darkness" ("White Greeks"). In "You Cry Because My Love Isn't Deeper, I Know" the dreamer compares himself with Titian, who supposedly "flew from one to / another among colors" until his last breath. "*Money Shots*" is supposedly inspired in part by some medieval Italian cult of perverse monks who practiced masturbation in front of holy icons. The urge to confess, to reveal all, remains.

In "Who Doesn't Hide behind the Altar" Šalamun writes: "I'm eternal, death says." Death embodies the imposed violence

---

6   Although upon closer consideration I might add that the mechanism Šalamun uses is a form of revealing the inherent violence of language, while neutralizing it through language, turning it into memory to be freely shared and passed on. Poetry is given to be given. Hannah Arendt's distinction in *On Violence* between power and violence is crucial, where there is violence/ coercion, there is no power: "Power springs up whenever people get together and act in concert, but it derives its legitimacy from the initial getting together rather than from any action that then may follow. . . .The point here is that violence itself is incapable of speech, and not merely that speech is helpless when confronted with violence."

7   See the poem: "Vzgoja Pesnika" ("The Education of the Poet"), *Praznik (Feast)*, 1976: "I am light, a small beam of light. / It's truly fantastic how stars eat me / More and more, what infinite food I am" (translation mine).

of life itself as the "never-ending cycle of collective murder"[8] into which we are born and have to face without end. Blood, sweat, spit, tears, and semen are the currencies of this world. All transmitted from skin to skin, organ to organ, power exchanges, pains of pleasures, a visceral brutal beauty which is both horror and growth, or growth through horror, transmuted, breathed through, both particle and wave, both past and future, both light. Šalamun does report on this.

If by revealing violence through language you reveal language as violence or reproduce violence through language—remains a crucial (and possibly unanswerable) question, as old as writing itself.

Although Šalamun is aware of the danger and unpredictability of conscious surrender to the unconscious forces of language, he cannot help himself not to produce these endless streams of images. He said many times, referring to his production: "I'm just giving out, printing this salad," implying he doesn't really know what it is and that he produces it as if it were a bodily function, as if constantly writing the act of writing itself.

Words, poems, books are seen as organic matter, a secretion, a discharge, holy excrement, sacred acts. The void, the space a poem creates, the consequence of the poem is the object of the poem. Šalamun's opus magnum is a writing out of, his books are cocoons, the skin he left behind, while he finally became what he wrote, he is, everywhere, everyone, and no one, present as a matter of code, downloaded and transformed with every download.

---

8   Werner Herzog in the documentary *The Burden of Dreams*, 1982.

ACKNOWLEDGMENTS

The poem *"Money Shots"* was first published as part of the Storylines exhibition at the Guggenheim Museum in New York City in summer 2015.

Grateful acknowledgement is made to the literary magazines *Jubilat* and *Transom*, which first published some of these poems in translation.

Black Ocean would like to thank Tibor Hrs Pandur, the Slovene poet, dramatist, translator and editor of the literary magazine IDIOT, for graciously providing the afterword.